P9-DGW-944

The Story of

GOLD

Hal Hellman

A FIRST BOOK

FRANKLIN WATTS
A Division of Grolier Publishing
New York London Hong Kong Sydney
Danbury, Connecticut

Chemical consultant: Geoffrey Buckwalter, Ph.D.
Cover design by Robin Hessel Hoffmann

Photographs copyright ©: North Wind Picture Archives: p. 7; Art Resource,
NY: pp. 8 (Erich Lessing), 23 (SEF), 27 (Scala); The Bettmann Archive: pp. 11,
17; Photo Researchers: pp. 13 (John G. Ross), 14 (Erich Schrempp), 32 (Dr.
Mitsuo Ohtsuki/SPL), 39 (Phillippe Plailly/SPL); Smithsonian Institution,
National Numismatic Collections: p. 18; Superstock: p. 21, 51; Comstock:
pp. 30, 47; Archive Photos: p. 43; Boltin Picture Library: p. 45; South Dakota
State Archives: p. 49; The Gold Institute: pp. 53, 55.

Library of Congress Cataloging-in-Publication Data

Hellman, Hal, 1927-
The Story of gold / by Hal Hellman.
p. cm. — (A First book)
Includes bibliographical references and index.
Summary: Discusses the nature of gold and the value of this metal throughout
history, as well as some of its uses and its role in the development of the science
of chemistry.
ISBN 0-531-20224-0
1. Gold—Juvenile literature. [1. Gold] I. Title. II. Series: First books.
TN761.6.H45   1966
669' .22—dc20   96-1246 CIP AC

Contents

Chapter 1

THE GOLDEN GOD

One day in 1799, twelve-year-old Conrad Reed found a treasure in a stream. Walking near his home in North Carolina, he saw a beautiful yellow rock the size of a baseball just waiting to be plucked from the water. When he carried it home, Conrad must have noticed that it was very heavy. Even so, neither he nor his family realized it was a nugget of gold.

After a few years, his family sold the rock to a jeweler for $3.50. Soon, the cry, "Gold! Gold's been found in North Carolina!" began spreading like wildfire across the young country. It was the first gold strike in the United States. Many more gold nuggets were dug from the North Carolina soil, some as big as grapefruits. Conrad's nugget,

5

weighing 17 pounds (almost 8 kilograms), eventually sold for $4,000.

When gold was discovered in Georgia in 1829, a stampede of people came from every state. They came on foot, on horseback—any which way they could. It was said that they acted more like crazy men than anything else.

In 1848, gold was discovered in California, and things got even crazier. Wild-eyed men with gold fever rushed there from other states and from all over the world. Some became rich, but many became disappointed and sick. Often they ended up poorer than when they began.

What is it about this shiny yellow metal that makes people act so crazy? What makes gold so valuable that people will risk what little money they have—and even their lives—to chase after it?

For one thing, gold is very rare. There is an average of only 10 pounds of gold for every 2 billion pounds of dirt on earth. All the gold in the world would probably make a cube only 60 feet (18 meters) on each side.

But gold is also very special in other ways. For instance, it is one of the few metals that doesn't rust or corrode. That's why it makes very beautiful, long-lasting jewelry. Gold is the only metal other than copper that has natural color. All other metals are gray or white. And no other metal can match gold's beautiful glow.

The unique qualities of gold have inspired people to seek it out for ages. To ancient peoples, the golden metal was like the sun. The Latin word for gold, *aurum*, means

Gold seekers crowded the streams of California in 1849.

A gold plate, made by Egyptians more than 1400 years B.C., has a sun at its center.

"shining dawn." Because gold is pure and everlasting like a god, ancient Egyptians thought of it as a symbol of their sun god.

Since that time, gold has been treated like a god in many other ways. It has been made into money and worshipped for the wealth it can provide. As in the gold rushes, people have often been willing to do anything to get it. Some even tried to change lead and other metals into gold.

In a way, many of these people were pursuing a false god—a god of greed. They were not even aware of the godlike qualities of gold. In their feverish attempts to get rich fast, they missed out on the beauty of the golden god.

Even though gold has been around for a very long time, only in this century have we gotten to know some of the scientific reasons for its magnificent qualities. We now understand what sets it apart from other substances.

Not only is gold beautiful, but it is a good conductor of electricity and a good reflector of light. These and other qualities have been put to work in a surprising variety of ways in electronics, medicine, space, and industry.

If you read on, you can get to know gold, too. You will find that it has brought people much pleasure and joy. But you will also see that it has caused a great deal of misery. By the time you finish reading, you will know much of what scientists know about this precious metal and all the ways it has affected the world.

This is the story of gold.

Chapter 2

ANCIENT GOLD

Even though gold is very rare, it was one of the first metals people discovered thousands of years ago. Its sparkling, yellow color is easy to see against the earth. And, unlike most other metals, pure gold can sometimes be found lying on the ground. That's because gold doesn't interact much with other substances.

Other metals, including silver and copper, interact with the air. They are slowly eaten away over time in a process called *corrosion.* They change color and lose their shine.

Gold is different. It tends to remain pure and unchanged. The first bit of gold taken out of the earth thousands of years ago is surely still around somewhere. And it is no doubt as shiny and bright now as it was then.

Silver earrings from about 600 B.C. have corroded,
but gold earrings from the same period look like new.

Even gold coins from sunken treasure ships shine and glitter, while the wood and the iron in the ship has rotted and rusted away.

As long as 6,000 years ago, people began finding gold and using it for decoration. When they saw how long it lasted, gold took on more meaning. It seemed to be like an everlasting god, so they began making golden objects for religious and magical purposes.

So the great rulers of the ancient world, especially the pharaohs of Egypt, saw gold as sacred. Gold came to symbolize the Egyptian sun god, Amon-Re, creator of all things. The Egyptians believed that anyone who had gold would have riches and eternal life.

To them, death was merely the beginning of a journey to another world. When pharaohs died, they were buried with whatever they might need in the next life. The tombs were filled with gold to make sure each pharoah would have a comfortable life as a ruler in the world beyond.

The tomb of the young king Tutankhamen, who died in 1350 B.C., is the most spectacular of those that have been discovered. In 1922, archaeologists found four large burial chambers so filled with golden treasures that it took years to catalog and remove them. His body was wrapped in gold and laid in three golden coffins, one inside the other. These coffins were then enclosed in a gold-covered shrine.

WORKING WITH GOLD

The goldsmiths who made the objects in King Tut's tomb were surprisingly skilled. Even before Egyptian times, people found ways to strengthen gold by melting and mixing it with other metals. This was important because pure gold is too soft to use in jewelry and objects of art. The Egyptians then improved the methods of mixing metals. Mixtures of metals are called *alloys*.

The Egyptians also found clever ways of forming gold into shapes. One is *gilding*, covering objects with a thin layer of gold. This process takes advantage of an unusual property of the precious metal. If you gently hammered a small

King Tut's golden throne shows the sun shining on him and his wife.

cube of gold, what do you think would happen? It is so soft that it would flatten out, without losing any of its luster.

And if you kept on hammering, you would eventually have a thin sheet of gold the size of a room. The process of hammering gold is known as *goldbeating*. The thin sheets of gold, called *gold leaf*, have a slight greenish tint. No other metal can be hammered and shaped as easily as gold. In other words, it is extremely *malleable*.

The Egyptians also found that a small cube of gold could be drawn out into very thin wire. If the wire was stretched very thin, it could extend 50 miles (80 kilometers). The Egyptians attached gold wire to a background of gold to make jewelry and decorations. This effect, called *filigree,* is still used in jewelry today.

Gold is so soft that it can be hammered into foil.

The goldsmiths came up with an ingenious way to make solid gold objects of any shape they desired. For instance, they could make complex, delicate items such as flowers out of gold. They first sculpted the object in wax and then covered it in modeling clay, leaving an opening at the top. After the clay hardened, molten gold was poured into the opening.

The gold was so hot that the wax melted and boiled away into the air. The gold cooled and hardened in the shape of the clay mold. When the clay was broken away, a perfect golden casting of the original wax item remained. People today use a similar process, called the lost wax method, to make intricate objects.

But it wasn't only the goldsmiths who were doing remarkable things in Egypt. Because Egyptians used so much gold, they worked hard to find better ways of getting it from the ground. Ancient Egypt was really the birthplace of gold mining.

Although gold can be found as nuggets or as flakes floating along in a stream, it is sometimes found mixed with other metals and minerals in the ground. It is still pure gold, but it is so thoroughly mixed that it is in tiny particles. The particles of gold are hidden, like salt in a mixture of flour and baking soda. Since gold is so rare, the Egyptians began trying to separate gold from these mixtures.

But it was hard to tell just by looking whether a piece of rocky material from the ground contained gold. They had to find ways to estimate the amount of gold in a sample of rock.

One method was to rub the sample on a black surface. From the color of the mark and the softness of the material, they could get a rough idea of how much gold it contained. If there was enough gold, they would mine the rock in the surrounding area.

As the pharaohs called for more and more gold, the miners were forced to mine areas containing less gold. To locate them, they had to actually separate the gold from a sample from the area. They then divided the weight of gold by the weight of the sample. This told them very precisely the percentage of gold that the area contained.

They developed a clever way of melting gold from the sample by grinding up the ore and heating it with some lead ore and sand. The same basic process, called a *fire assay*, is used by mining companies today. It is so accurate that it routinely measures as little as an ounce of gold in a ton of ore.

It is also the same basic process used to get the gold from the ore. The Egyptian fire assay, however, was not as advanced as the modern method. If there was silver in the ore, it would melt and mix with the gold. The Egyptians thought this mixture, called *electrum*, was a completely different metal from both gold and silver. It was really a gold-silver alloy.

The Egyptians considered electrum quite beautiful in its own way. The silver lightened the color of the gold and strengthened it, too. Queen Hatshepsut, the only woman pharoah of Egypt, powdered her cheeks with a dust of electrum.

This drawing shows ancient Egyptians carrying out a fire assay.

A MEDIUM OF EXCHANGE

Eventually other civilizations began to rise and flourish around Egypt. Among them was a city-state called Lydia, located in what is now western Turkey. As in Egypt, the rulers of Lydia collected fabulous riches in gold. Then, around 560 B.C., they came up with a clever idea. They made coins out of gold and used them to buy things.

The coins were weighed carefully and given a particular value based on the amount of gold they contained. The gold was probably mixed with a little silver and perhaps another metal. Pure gold would have been too soft to withstand the handling that coins get. They would have been scratched and bent too easily.

The first coins were made in the seventh century B.C.

This simple idea had an enormous impact on the business world. Instead of having to trade one thing for another, merchants had a convenient, more organized way to pay for things.

The idea of trading with gold coins spread very rapidly worldwide. Later, when the Romans became powerful and took over much of the ancient world, Roman gold coins were accepted and admired everywhere.

In the fourth century A.D., the Greeks used the tiny seeds of the carob tree as weights on a scale balance to precisely determine the amount of gold in their coins. The weight of 24 carob seeds equaled the weight of a small pure-gold coin.

The same unit is used today to indicate the purity of gold. It is called a *karat*, from the Greek word for carob. Pure gold is 24-karat gold. When jewelry is made of an alloy that is only half gold, it is called 12-karat gold.

Not long after coins were invented, con artists began making fake coins. They could easily cover a cheap metal with a thin layer of gold to make it look like solid gold. Or they might make an alloy of gold with copper or zinc and pass it off as solid gold.

The transformation of gold into money made people want it even more. Some of them would do anything—lie, cheat, or steal—to get it. People began to seek it for its buying power, not just for its beauty, purity, and magic. The golden god was becoming a god of money.

Chapter 3

THE MAGIC OF GOLD

The Egyptian goldsmiths were very skilled, but they did not understand how or why their processes worked. For all they knew, it could be magic. When the ancient Greeks saw the Egyptians work with gold for the first time, they must have been filled with wonder.

Not long after that, in about the third century A.D., the Greeks began to look for a way to change other metals into gold. Perhaps the Egyptian processes inspired them. After all, the Egyptians could make the gold in an alloy travel to the surface and completely cover it. It must have looked like the alloy was being changed into pure gold!

The idea fit in very well with the Greek theories about *matter,* the stuff that makes up everything on earth.

Back then, the Greeks believed that metals slowly grew in the ground, changing from one into another until they reached perfection.

Perfection, of course, was gold. The metals started out black, and then turned white, and finally, gold. Perhaps the Greeks thought that the Egyptian processes were just speeding up the growth of the metals.

The Greeks also believed it was possible to change one substance into any other substance. All you had to do was adjust the amounts of the four basic substances that made it up. These substances were earth, air, fire, and water. The Greeks believed that these four *elements* were part of everything on earth.

So it is no wonder that the Greeks became convinced there was a way to turn metals into gold. Besides, gold had

The Greeks believed that gold grew in the ground.

a touch of magic about it even after it came to be used in everyday trading.

Like the Egyptians before them, the Greeks associated gold with the sun. They believed in astrology, the idea that the movements of the sun, the moon, and the planets control events on earth. Since the sun is the most powerful of these bodies, gold was thought to have power, too. They thought it could heal the sick and lead to everlasting life.

The quest to turn metals such as lead, tin, or copper into gold is known as *alchemy*. The alchemists sought not just incredible riches but also spiritual perfection.

Because gold is so pure, it seemed to have a quality of goodness about it. It avoided interacting with lesser metals or materials. This seemed a lot like people's religious attempts to remain good and pure by avoiding bad influences. The alchemists believed that if they found a way to turn other metals into gold, they too could achieve goodness in the process.

The Chinese began pursuing a spiritual kind of alchemy even before the Greeks. They searched for a substance that was so charged with mystical power that it would adjust the qualities of a metal or a person to perfection. They called it the *elixir of life* because they believed it would make people live forever.

Arabs, who traded with both the Greeks and the Chinese, began looking for the elixir of life around A.D. 700. They experimented with many substances in their search. To test each one, they tried mixing it with different metals.

Arabs practiced alchemy long before Europeans did.

They hoped that one of the substances would adjust the elements in the metals to the perfect combination for gold. Anything that moved a gray metal closer to the yellow of the golden god encouraged them to believe that they were on the right track.

In about A.D. 1200, Europeans picked up the Arabian ideas and began their own studies of alchemy. The word *alchemy* comes from an Arab word, and that word might have come from the Chinese word for gold—*kim*.

THE FRUITS OF ALCHEMY

The Europeans set up laboratories and began studying substances of all kinds. They found that when some substances combined, they would sizzle, give off fumes, or even explode. These strange chemical reactions produced new substances in place of the old. They gave the alchemists hope that they would someday hit upon the combination that would produce gold.

During their searches, Arabian and European alchemists discovered many new chemicals. An alchemist produced the first substance to glow in the dark. Today it is called barium sulfide. Alchemists also discovered a whole new group of chemicals called *acids*. When an acid is added to a metal, such as tin, the tin dissolves, leaving a powdery substance. They discovered powerful acids, which we know today as nitric, hydrochloric, and sulfuric acids.

After searching and searching, they found only one acid that would dissolve gold. It was a mixture of nitric and hydrochloric acids. They called it *aqua regia*, which is Latin for "royal water."

But the alchemists never did find a way to make gold. Plenty of them claimed they had in order to trick people out of their money. These sneaky alchemists might stir their pot of chemicals with a stick containing gold hidden inside. As the pot warmed up, the gold would suddenly appear. Or they might create a substance that looked like gold.

Since people believed that metals grew in the ground like plants, tricksters often tried selling "seeds" of gold. When placed on a gray metal, the seeds would supposedly gradually change it to gold.

Because of these tricks, alchemy eventually got a bad name. After alchemists were discovered making fake gold coins in 1317, the pope of the French Catholic Church ordered all alchemists to leave France. And in 1403, England passed a law forbidding attempts to make gold with seeds.

By the early 1500s, Paracelsus, a famous alchemist and doctor, began shifting the focus of alchemy. He argued that alchemists should study the reactions between all kinds of chemicals, not just those that might lead to gold. If they did that, he thought, new medicines could be discovered.

As a result, alchemists began studying chemistry for its own sake. By the seventeenth century, the goal of alchemy had moved almost completely away from changing metals into gold and toward achieving spiritual perfection. But many alchemists still believed that when they achieved spiritual perfection, they would then be able to change metals into gold.

A great physicist named Isaac Newton explored alchemy as a kind of religion during this time. In fact, he spent more time in his alchemical laboratory than he did on the laws of motion and gravity that made him famous. Some people believe that his work with alchemy helped him come up with those laws.

THE END OF ALCHEMY

Alchemy gradually died out, but the laboratory methods, equipment, and chemicals became the basis for a new science—chemistry. Chemical experiments led scientists to begin questioning the theory of the four elements.

The Greeks didn't think it was important to do experiments to back up their theories. But now scientists realized that theories must be checked by testing real substances.

One of the first to criticize the Greek's four-element theory was an English chemist named Robert Boyle. In 1658, he pointed out that many, many experiments had been done to try to break gold into its four elements. In all those experiments, he said, no one had found even one of the four elements in gold. It was time, he argued, to admit that something was wrong with the theory.

Over the next century, scientists found more and more evidence that air and earth could be broken down into other substances. If they were made of other substances, how could they be elements? Air, for instance, is actually a mixture of invisible *gases* such as oxygen.

After investigating these and other new gases, a French chemist named Antoine Lavoisier discovered that even water is not an element. It is made of oxygen and another invisible gas called hydrogen. Finally, the world realized that the Greeks had been completely wrong about the elements. Hydrogen and oxygen were the real elements, not water, air, earth, or fire.

Alchemists developed laboratory methods and equipment
that were later used in chemistry.

In 1789, Lavoisier listed 33 substances that he considered elements because they had not been broken down into anything else. Of course, gold was among them. So were all the other metals, including copper, iron, lead, silver, and tin.

This was the beginning of modern chemistry. Scientists realized that the strange reactions between substances that the alchemists first observed were simply elements joining together to create *compounds*. In some cases, compounds were separating into their elements.

When aqua regia dissolved gold, for instance, a chemical reaction was taking place. Gold was actually forming a compound with one of the elements in aqua regia. Even the corrosion of copper and other metals turned out to be a chemical reaction. Oxygen from the air combines chemically with the metal and forms a powdery compound.

Chemists went on to discover more and more elements. They found a total of 92 elements that occur naturally in the world. And they have been able to make others artificially in laboratories.

So even though the quest to change metals into gold failed, alchemy set the stage for a revolution. This revolution eventually resulted in chemistry as we know it today. In the end, the world got something much more valuable than gold: the truth about the incredible way matter interacts in our world. And we have gold to thank for that.

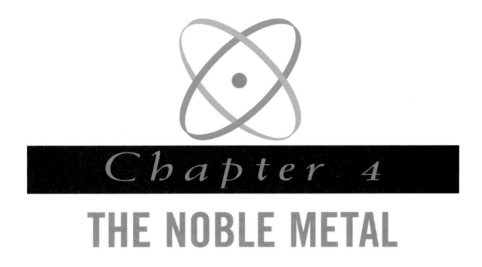

Chapter 4

THE NOBLE METAL

In the new field of chemistry, gold was no longer in the spotlight. It was just one of more than two dozen other elements, no better or worse than the rest. But each element had its own unique characteristics, just as people have their own special personalities.

Chemists tried to learn everything they could about each of the elements and how they behave. They began to find out the elements' *properties*. As they did, they discovered what made gold seem so special throughout history.

By comparing the elements with one another, chemists began to organize them into groups. Gold belonged to a large group of elements that had always been known as metals. They tended to be shiny, dense

Like other metals, gold is very shiny.

materials. Before long, chemists began to find out some very interesting things about metals. For one thing, if two different metals were placed next to each other, electricity would flow between them!

At that time, electricity was a strange and wondrous thing. It had only recently been discovered. No one knew exactly what it was or what caused it.

Chemists tried passing electricity through many different materials. They found that metals carry electricity better than any other group. And gold turned out to be one of the best electrical conductors of all.

But scientists did not discover what electricity was until the end of the nineteenth century. That's when J. J. Thomson, an English physicist, realized that it consists of tiny particles flowing through a substance. These particles, which were soon named *electrons,* each have a negative electrical charge.

Metals are good conductors because of their ability to carry a larger flow of electrons than other materials. But where do these electrons come from?

Chemists started to find the answer earlier in the 1800s as they tried to understand how elements bond with one another. They discovered that elements form chemical compounds because they have an electrical attraction for each other.

Elements contain particles called *atoms* that can become electrically charged. The atoms from one element bond with another element as a result of their electrical charges. The atoms gather in groups called *molecules.*

Thomson realized that electrons must be partly responsible for the electrical charges on atoms. The electrons had to come from inside atoms. And he was right.

Electrons make up the outer part of an atom. The center of the atom, called the *nucleus,* contains particles with a positive charge, called *protons.* They are attracted to electrons because they have opposite electrical charges. The simplest atom is the hydrogen atom with only one proton with one electron moving around it.

Each element has an atom with its own special number of protons and electrons. Oxygen has 8 protons and 8 electrons. But gold has a whopping 79 protons and 79 electrons!

The number of protons in an atom is called the *atomic number*. In nature, there is an element for every atomic number from 1 to 92. So you can see that gold has one of the highest atomic numbers of any element.

Compared to electrons, protons are very heavy; they weigh 1,836 times as much as electrons. Another particle in gold's nucleus weighs slightly more than a proton. It is called the *neutron* because it has a neutral electrical charge. A single gold atom has 118 neutrons and 79 protons in its nucleus. That makes it one of the heaviest atoms. Its *atomic weight* is 197.

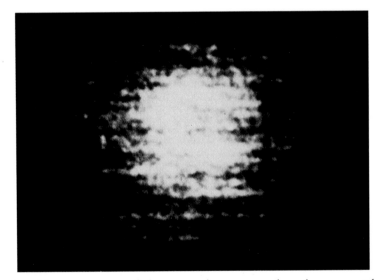

A gold atom is one of the atoms large enough to be seen with very powerful microscopes. It is multiplied here 30 million times.

What is more, gold atoms, like those of most metals, are packed very closely together. As a result, gold has one of the highest densities of the elements. Its density is something people immediately notice when they pick up a piece of gold. A tiny cubic inch (about 16 cubic cm) of gold weighs more than two thirds of a pound (almost a third of a kilogram).

THE PURITY OF GOLD

Electrons, on the outer part of an atom, determine how atoms interact with one another. Gold's tendency to remain pure can be explained by the position of its 79 electrons. They are arranged in six rings, or *shells*, surrounding the nucleus.

Each shell is a home for a family of electrons. The electrons in the outer shell may occasionally be attracted to the protons of another atom. If the families in both outer shells get along, the atoms may decide to bond and make one big happy family.

But that doesn't happen too often when gold is involved. The family of electrons in its outer shell is usually perfectly satisfied being on its own. To understand why, you must first know more about why other elements bond.

Hydrogen and oxygen bond to each other to make one of earth's most common compounds—water. Hydrogen has only 1 lonely electron in a single shell. In all other atoms, the shell closest to the nucleus houses a family of 2 electrons.

Periodic Table

1 H 1.00794 Hydrogen								
3 **Li** 6.941 Lithium	**4** **Be** 9.01218 Beryllium							
11 **Na** 22.98977 Sodium	**12** **Mg** 24.305 Magnesium			METALS				
19 **K** 39.0983 Potassium	**20** **Ca** 40.078 Calcium	**21** **Sc** 44.95591 Scandium	**22** **Ti** 47.88 Titanium	**23** **V** 50.9415 Vanadium	**24** **Cr** 51.9161 Chromium	**25** **Mn** 54.93805 Manganese	**26** **Fe** 55.847 Iron	**27** **Co** 58.9332 Cobalt
37 **Rb** 85.4678 Rubidium	**38** **Sr** 87.62 Strontium	**39** **Y** 88.9059 Yttrium	**40** **Zr** 91.224 Zirconium	**41** **Nb** 92.9064 Niobium	**42** **Mo** 95.94 Molybdenum	**43** **Tc** (98) Technetium	**44** **Ru** 101.07 Ruthenium	**45** **Rh** 102.9055 Rhodium
55 **Cs** 132.9054 Cesium	**56** **Ba** 137.327 Barium	**57** * **La** 138.9055 Lanthanum	**72** **Hf** 178.49 Hafnium	**73** **Ta** 180.9479 Tantalum	**74** **W** 183.85 Tungsten	**75** **Re** 186.207 Rhenium	**76** **Os** 190.2 Osmium	**77** **Ir** 192.22 Iridium
87 **Fr** (223) Francium	**88** **Ra** 226.025 Radium	**89** ** **Ac** (227) Actinium	**104** **Unq** (261)† (Unnilquadium)	**105** **Unp** (262)† (Unnilpentium)	**106** **Unh** (263)† (Unnilhoxium)	**107** **Uns** (262)† (Unnilseptium)	**108** **Uno** (265)† (Unniloctium)	**109** **Une** (266)† (Unnilnonium)

58 Ce 140.115 Cerium	59 Pr 140.9077 Praseodymium	60 Nd 144.24 Neodymium	61 Pm (145) Promethium	62 Sm 150.36 Samarium
90 **Th** 232.0381 Thorium	**91** **Pa** 231.0359 Protactinium	**92** **U** 238.029 Uranium	**93** **Np** 237.048 Neptunium	**94** **Pu** (244) Plutonium

At atomic number 79, gold (Au) is one of the heaviest of the elements. It is a member of the large group of metallic elements.

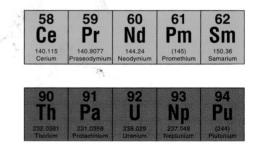

of the Elements

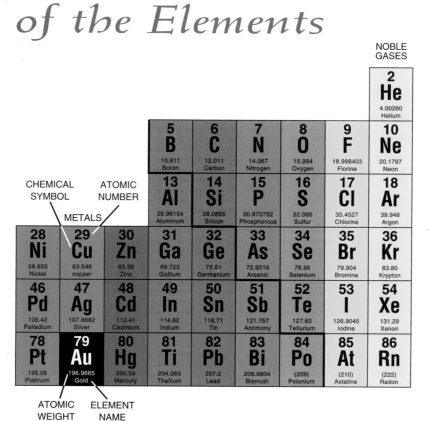

NOBLE
GASES

					2 **He** 4.00260 Helium
5 **B** 10.811 Boron	**6** **C** 12.011 Carbon	**7** **N** 14.067 Nitrogen	**8** **O** 15.994 Oxygen	**9** **F** 18.998403 Florine	**10** **Ne** 20.1797 Neon
13 **Al** 26.96154 Aluminum	**14** **Si** 28.0855 Silicon	**15** **P** 30.973762 Phosphorous	**16** **S** 32.066 Sulfur	**17** **Cl** 35.4527 Chlorine	**18** **Ar** 39.948 Argon

CHEMICAL SYMBOL — ATOMIC NUMBER — METALS

28 **Ni** 58.693 Nickel	**29** **Cu** 63.546 copper	**30** **Zn** 65.39 Zinc	**31** **Ga** 69.723 Gallium	**32** **Ge** 72.61 Germanium	**33** **As** 72.9216 Arsenic	**34** **Se** 78.96 Selenium	**35** **Br** 79.904 Bromine	**36** **Kr** 83.80 Krypton
46 **Pd** 106.42 Palladium	**47** **Ag** 107.8682 Silver	**48** **Cd** 112.41 Cadmium	**49** **In** 114.82 Indium	**50** **Sn** 118.71 Tin	**51** **Sb** 121.757 Antimony	**52** **Te** 127.60 Tellurium	**53** **I** 126.9045 Iodine	**54** **Xe** 131.29 Xenon
78 **Pt** 195.08 Platinum	**79** **Au** 196.9665 Gold	**80** **Hg** 200.59 Mercury	**81** **Ti** 204.383 Thallium	**82** **Pb** 207.2 Lead	**83** **Bi** 208.9804 Bismuth	**84** **Po** (209) Polonium	**85** **At** (210) Astatine	**86** **Rn** (222) Radon

ATOMIC WEIGHT — ELEMENT NAME

63 **Eu** 151.965 Europium	**64** **Gd** 157.25 Gadolinium	**65** **Tb** 158.9253 Terbium	**66** **Dy** 162.50 Dysprosium	**67** **Ho** 164.9303 Holmium	**68** **Er** 167.26 Erbium	**69** **Tm** 168.9342 Thulium	**70** **Yb** 173.04 Ytterbiium	**71** **Lu** 174.967 Lutetium

95 **Am** (243) Americium	**96** **Cm** (247) Berkelium	**97** **Bk** (247) Berkelium	**98** **Cf** (251) Californium	**99** **Es** (252) Einsteinium	**100** **Fm** (257) Fermium	**101** **Md** (258) Mendelevium	**102** **No** (259) Nobelium	**103** **Lr** (260) Lawrencium

The invisible gas helium, for instance, has 2 electrons in its only shell. Its family is complete, so it doesn't bond with other atoms. But the hydrogen atom tries to bond with other atoms that will welcome its electron into their families. That's why it bonds with oxygen.

Oxygen has a complete first family of 2 electrons and a second family of 6 electrons in a "house" or shell, farther away from the nucleus. But the second family is not complete until it has 8 electrons. So oxygen bonds with atoms that can share 2 electrons.

Two hydrogen atoms can supply the electrons oxygen needs. The chemical formula for water, H_2O, shows that each molecule contains 2 hydrogen atoms and 1 oxygen atom.

Chlorine is another element that bonds with hydrogen. It has 17 electrons in three shells. Its first two shells are completely filled, with 2 and 8 electrons. The third shell, with 7 electrons, needs 1 more to make a complete family. So 1 chlorine atom bonds with 1 hydrogen atom to make hydrochloric acid. Its chemical formula is HCl.

With six shells, the gold atom is much more complicated than these atoms. The fourth, fifth, and sixth shells each have room for 8 electrons, plus 10 more. It's as if the families in these houses have each added on a wing with five extra bedrooms, and each bedroom can hold 2 electrons.

The sixth shell has a second wing with seven bedrooms that can hold 14 more electrons. Gold's outer shell contains a total of 25 electrons. One electron stays in the master bedroom of the main house and the rest completely fill the bedrooms in the two wings.

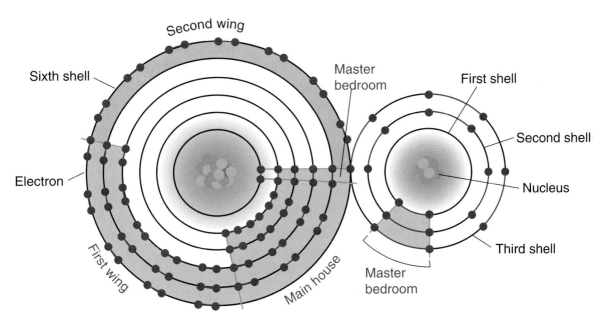

Second wing

Sixth shell

Master
bedroom

First shell

Second shell

Electron

Nucleus

First wing

Third shell

Main house

Master
bedroom

GOLD ATOM   CHLORINE ATOM

A gold atom with six families, or shells, of electrons bonds with a
chlorine atom missing one electron in its third shell.

In most elements with at least four shells, the first 2 electrons in the outer shell stay in the master bedroom. But in gold, the electrons prefer to fill the two wings. It's as if they wanted to at least complete two small family groups in the outer shell rather than filling the master bedroom. Completing the two small groups seems to have a similar effect to filling the outer shell completely.

Because gold does not usually form bonds with other elements, it is called a noble metal. This suggests it is like members of royalty who do not marry commoners. Helium and other gases with completely filled outer shells are called noble gases for the same reason.

Copper, with four shells, and silver, with five shells, are also noble metals. Each has in its outer shell one electron in the master bedroom and a wing of five filled bedrooms. These two metals don't react with other elements much, but they do not remain as pure as gold.

GOLD'S BEST FRIEND

It may happen rarely, but gold does sometimes bond with other atoms. It seems that the electron in the master bedroom gets lonely and occasionally goes to stay with another atom's family. Chlorine is a favorite of gold's because it needs just 1 electron to complete its family.

One atom of gold bonds with 1 atom of chlorine in gold chloride. The chemical symbol for gold is Au, which comes from *aurum*, the Latin word for gold. The formula for gold chloride is AuCl.

But things can get more complicated. An atom of gold also sometimes bonds with 3 chlorine atoms. This compound is called gold trichloride. It seems as though the gold atom ships off a pair of electrons from the first wing to accompany the single electron from the master bedroom. Each electron fills an opening in a chlorine atom.

It is not completely clear why gold varies the number of electrons it shares. Hydrogen, oxygen, and other elements with small atomic numbers tend to be more consistent. The outer electrons in metals aren't held very tightly in position, partly because they are farther from the nucleus than the electrons of hydrogen and oxygen. All metals have at least three shells of electrons.

Some of the outer electrons in metals can actually break free of the atoms. These electrons flow as a stampede of electricity when any area of the metal has more of a positive charge than where they are.

Electricity is actually the movement of an *electron cloud.* In a group of metal atoms, the outer electrons break free and form an electron cloud surrounding the atoms. The negatively charged electron cloud acts as a kind of "glue" that holds the positively charged metal atoms together.

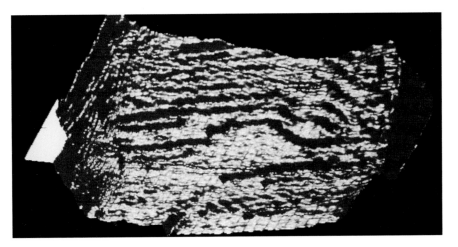

You can see layers of gold atoms in this image of a thin film of gold. A very powerful microscope interacts with the electron cloud of the gold film to produce the image.

Gold is a good conductor of electricity because the electron in the master bedroom can break free of its atom so easily and because its outer shell has space for traveling electrons. The electrons in the wing with five bedrooms cannot always break free, but their loose connection to the atom aids the flow of electricity.

The glue provided by the electron cloud makes most metals strong and dense. It's the reason the atoms pack together so closely. Even though the glue is strong, metal atoms can slide past each other fairly easily. So when the metal is hammered, it bends or flattens rather than breaking. This is particularly true of gold.

The cloud of electrons also makes metals shiny. The electrons absorb incoming light at the metal's surface and reflect it all at once across the surface. If it were not for the electron cloud, the metal atoms would simply absorb the light.

Most metal atoms do not bond with the atoms of other metals. The atoms mix together like the ingredients in a cake batter, but their electrons don't interact. Alloys of different metals are simply mixtures of atoms.

After chemists discovered all these incredible things about elements and the particles that make them up, alchemy seemed very foolish indeed. There was obviously no way to change the number of protons in atoms by mixing or bonding them with the atoms of another substance. But a different sort of alchemy was soon discovered near the beginning of the twentieth century.

NATURE'S ALCHEMY

Not long after J. J. Thomson discovered the electron, chemists made another astounding discovery. They found that some elements continually release particles and energy. These elements are *radioactive*.

They release *beta particles*, which are electrons, and *alpha particles*, which are atomic nuclei containing two protons and two neutrons. Because they are losing protons, radioactive elements change, or decay, into other elements. They do naturally what the alchemists tried for so long to achieve.

Unfortunately, no element naturally decays into gold. But scientists have been able to make gold in the laboratory. In 1941, Harvard scientists converted mercury to gold by bombarding mercury atoms with high-speed neutrons. In a few of the mercury atoms, a speeding neutron penetrated the nucleus and converted it to a radioactive form of gold.

Mercury was chosen because it has only one more proton than gold. It is interesting that mercury was a favorite material of the alchemists, too. Lead, another favorite of theirs, has also been artificially converted to gold.

Most of this artificial gold decays rapidly into other elements. The longest-lasting form of gold has a half-life of only 186 days. What is more, it would cost something like a billion dollars to produce a pound (half a kilogram) of gold this way.

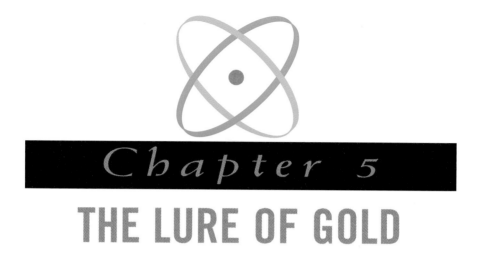

Chapter 5

THE LURE OF GOLD

The gleam of gold drew many explorers to new lands. Christopher Columbus was the most famous. Before discovering America, he caught gold fever when he saw the metal being mined along the Gold Coast of Africa.

Many historians believe that his real reason for sailing west from Spain for the Orient was to find gold.

Columbus was sent back with directions to settle the new land and start a gold mine. As he explored new areas, he kept his eye out for gold. When it was found, Columbus and the Spanish settlers often mistreated the natives to get it.

Over the next century, many more European explorers set out to find gold in the Americas. They were convinced that there existed somewhere in South America a land filled with gold and riches. They called it "El Dorado," which is Spanish for "the gilded one."

Francisco Pizarro must have thought he had found El Dorado when he arrived in the land of the Incas in 1531. The Incas were Native Americans living in what is now Peru.

Pizarro prepares his men to enter the capital city of the Incas.

To Pizarro's men, the Incan cities seemed to be filled with gold. Even the pipes that carried water in the palace in the capital city of Cuzco were made of gold.

But most of the gold was in the form of statues, jewelry, and other items. They were made by the same lost wax method used by the Egyptians. The Incas had developed it on their own.

They did some surprisingly advanced chemical work as well. Recent research by a scientist from the Massachusetts Institute of Technology indicates that some of the Incas' pieces were gilded with an incredibly thin layer of gold. The Incas were able to achieve the same quality as the modern method, which is called *electroplating*.

It's likely that the Incas' chemical technique originated with an even earlier civilization. The Chimu empire in Peru flourished between 1150 and 1450. Chimu goldsmiths mastered not only gold plating, but welding, making alloys, and lost wax casting.

To plate objects, they first coated them with an alloy of 30 percent gold and 70 percent copper. Then they applied acids extracted from plants. The copper reacted with the acids to form a compound called copper oxide. This oxide could be cleaned off to leave a thin layer of pure gold.

The Incas conquered the Chimu people and learned their goldsmithing skills. And they added considerable artistic talent of their own. But when the Spanish conquered the Incas, all they wanted was the gold. They had no interest in the Incas' artistry.

*A gold necklace made by the Incas in the 1400s is one of the
few pieces that survived the Spanish conquest.*

The Spanish melted down about 13 tons of golden
objects. Since gold has a relatively low melting point, it
was easy for them to do. By this simple act, a great cultur-
al treasure was lost forever.

SETTLING THE WEST

Gold was undoubtedly a major factor in the rapid settling of the American West. The lure of gold in California drew thousands upon thousands of people into what had been pure wilderness until then.

These people were the prospectors we see in movies and read about in books. The word *prospect* has to do with expectation and hope; and for many of them, that's all they had.

All a person needed to search for gold was a pick, a shovel, and a pie-shaped pan. Once prospectors found a stream, they could go right to work, looking for a jackpot in scoops from the streambed.

Because it is so dense, gold often settles in flakes in the bottom of streams. The flakes come from the wearing away of gold buried deep in the ground. In a method called panning, prospectors scooped up some sand, gravel, and water from the stream in a pie-shaped pan. They swished it around, swirling the water and dirt out of the pan. Tiny flakes of yellow metal remained behind in the bottom of the pan.

Many people who arrived in the first year of the gold rush—1848—did indeed make fortunes. But the 250,000 or so people who arrived from all parts of the world in 1849 and the following three years were not so lucky. Most of them ended up working for days' wages in miserable jobs. Gambling halls and saloons did big business.

In gold panning, flakes of gold settle to the bottom of the pan after material is scooped from a streambed.

Many of the gold diggers, or Forty-niners, as they were called, were thieves, gamblers, and outlaws.

In the last half of the nineteenth century, gold was discovered in other western states, too. In the 1870s, General George Armstrong Custer reported finding gold nuggets in South Dakota on land set aside for the Sioux Indians. The land, in the Black Hills, was sacred to the Sioux. By law, white men were not supposed to set foot on the reservation. But gold fever took hold, and local officials looked the other way when white men trespassed on the reservation.

Deadwood Gulch started out as a place along a stream where gold was found in the Black Hills. But it quickly grew into a wild, thundering mining town of 25,000 people.

Wild Bill Hickok, who became famous as a lawman in Kansas, went to Deadwood Gulch to search for gold after his career was over. Like so many others, he spent more time in the gambling hall than looking for gold. He was murdered while playing poker there in 1876. The town was also home to other legends of the American West, including Deadwood Dick and Calamity Jane.

Some people give gold credit for settling new lands, including Australia, Canada, and Alaska. But others say it was not worth the tragic effects the greed for gold had on native populations and other people. Gold expert Robert Boyle has written that the quest for gold led to "the vilest treatment of men ever devised."

Gold strikes still happen in modern times. But the stampedes of the nineteenth century are gone forever. The places where gold is easily retrieved have, for the most part, been found. And only mining companies have the technology to dredge up huge amounts of earth for very tiny amounts of gold. As many as 15 tons of rock may

Deadwood Gulch attracted throngs of gold diggers.

have to be taken from the earth to yield a single ounce of gold.

The greed for gold continues to have tragic results, but the main victim is the environment. Gold mining gouges out the land and increases erosion. And since chemicals are used to extract the gold from the rock, great quantities of mined rock must be disposed of as toxic waste.

The world's largest deposit of gold is in the rain forests of New Guinea. More than 100,000 tons of waste from gold mining is dumped into local rivers every day. Not only is the waste killing fish and other animals, but it is destroying the home of a Stone Age tribe called the Amungme.

Most of the world's gold comes from South Africa and Russia. Only a small percent of it comes from the United States and Canada. But there are still people who pan for gold in streams with some success. Their numbers increase whenever the price of gold rises.

GOOD AS GOLD

As a result of the gold rushes of the nineteenth century, many countries around the world began adopting a *gold standard*. This meant they guaranteed that their money was backed by a certain amount of gold in the country's treasury. Citizens could trade in money for gold whenever they wanted to.

The ancient cultures that used gold coins had the first real gold standards. By the early nineteenth century, most countries used silver coins and backed their paper money with silver. But when gold became more plentiful, it took over as the standard.

In the United States the gold standard fell apart in the Great Depression of the 1930s. Panicked citizens tried redeeming their money for gold in droves. Banks were unable to fill all the requests. So in 1934, the United States ended the gold standard and made it illegal for people to own monetary gold. The government gathered all the gold money in the country and stored it at Fort Knox in Kentucky.

In 1975 it became legal to own gold again. People bought so much gold that its price rose to $620 an ounce by 1980. It had been only $35 an ounce in 1970.

Many people invested in gold coins as a safeguard against economic calamity and they continue to do so today. They know that paper dollars can go down in value because of inflation, but gold will always be valuable simply because it's gold.

At the beginning of the twentieth century, many countries issued gold coins. They backed their paper money with gold bricks, or bullion.

In modern times, people have found a great variety of uses for gold besides money. Both industry and medicine have applications for gold trichloride dissolved in water. This liquid solution is useful in plating metals and as a medicine, too. In 1890, for example, a German physician used gold solutions to treat tuberculosis, a serious and common disease at the time.

A decade later, physicians found that gold solutions actually didn't do much for tuberculosis. But the solutions did seem to relieve pain in patients who had a kind of arthritis. Today, when all else fails, gold trichloride is still used as a treatment for rheumatoid arthritis. But the medical people don't know how it works.

Doctors also use gold compounds in special cases of ulcers, cancer, heart trouble, and even some forms of mental illness. So the alchemists were at least somewhat right about gold's healing abilities. Ancient Chinese acupuncturists used golden needles because of this, and some modern acupuncturists still use them.

Most applications of gold today have to do with its ability to conduct electricity. Its use in electronics actually began with a printing process. In 1903, a gold-based ink was developed as a way of printing gold decoration and art on books and other surfaces.

Later the method was used in *printed circuits*, electrical circuits printed on boards. The ink for printed circuits actually contains an alloy of gold with either nickel or silver. It is used on electrical contacts, where two components touch to make an electrical connection. Gold is the

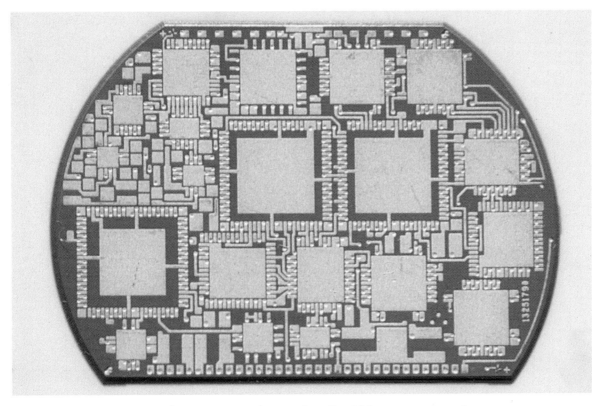

This printed circuit is made entirely of gold because it must be very reliable. It is part of a United States weapon called the Stinger missile.

ideal contact material because it conducts electricity so well and resists corrosion.

Gold contacts were used to assemble the world's very first *transistor*. A transistor is the basic electrical component of computers and other electronics. Today, the electronics industry is a major user of gold: over 95 percent of all elec-

53

trical contacts in computers and integrated circuits are gold-coated to ensure the highest reliability.

Gold-coated contacts are also used in air bags, safety devices put in many cars. When a sensor detects an impact, the bag inflates as a cushion to keep the driver from hitting the windshield. The sensor contacts must be made of gold to keep air bags working reliably for 10 to 15 years.

Gold is used even more extensively in the circuits that amplify signals from satellites and distant spacecraft. Since the signals are so weak, they must be amplified billions of times. Any corrosion or impurity in the circuit could destroy the signal.

Gold's talent for reflecting light is put to use in space equipment. Powerful radiation from the sun bombards astronauts and space equipment because there is no atmosphere for protection. A thin film of gold coats helmets, visors, tether lines, rocket engines and electronic systems.

Gold is such a marvelous reflector that a film a mere 6 millionths of an inch thin is enough to deflect the burning heat of the sun. Yet this is thin enough to allow the astronaut to see through a gold-coated visor.

The tinted windows of many new high-rise buildings may also contain gold. The tinted coating not only cuts down on the sun's glare, but it keeps out the heat, too. Thus, less air-conditioning is needed, and the amount of light entering the building does not change.

Another kind of gold film is used in high-security buildings to shield against electronic signals that enemies may be sending for spying purposes.

A thin film of gold on this firefighter's visor reflects light and protects him from intense heat.

The reflecting ability of gold is put to work in the linings of industrial ovens to keep heat in and save energy.

Gold films protect electronic circuitry boxes from cosmic and solar radiation bursts. This radiation can cause such delicate electronics to fail.

The chemistry of gold itself is taking a surprising new turn. Most metals can act as *catalysts,* helping chemical reactions happen faster or slower. Because gold is such an unreactive material, chemists never thought of using it as a catalyst. But researchers at Pennsylvania State University have found a way.

If very tiny specks of gold are deposited onto a material called titanium dioxide, it seems to act as an excellent catalyst for some important reactions. For instance, it can help convert poisonous carbon monoxide to carbon dioxide.

Gold's resistance to chemical change has been particularly useful in an area of dentistry called tooth restoration. Most dental fillings are made of an alloy of silver and mercury. Since the alloy can gradually corrode, gold is used when an entire tooth must be replaced. Worldwide, dentists use almost two million ounces of gold for this purpose every year.

To make the filling look like a tooth, dentists coat the gold with porcelain—a hard, enamel-like material. But in some countries, especially in South America, a smile that features gold fillings and even gold-capped teeth is something to be proud of.

So even today gold represents the ultimate in beauty, wealth, and perfection. In classrooms, everyone knows that the gold star is the best. In the Olympics, the athletes strive for the gold medal to show that they are at the top of their sport in the world. And couples give each other gold wedding rings to symbolize a marriage that will last forever.

History has taught us that if greed enters in, gold can bring out the worst in people. But, as the true alchemists knew, the golden god also has the power to inspire us to be the best we can be.

Glossary

alchemy—a practice in which people experimented with chemicals to find a way to change gray metals into gold and to cure diseases.

alloy—a mixture of two or more metals. The atoms of the various metals remain separate from each other.

aqua regia—the only acid that will dissolve gold. It is composed of one part concentrated nitric acid and three parts hydrochloric acid.

atomic number—the number of protons in the nucleus of an atom. This number identifies the element and indicates its place in the periodic table of the elements.

atomic weight—the average mass of atoms of an element relative to some standard, usually carbon-12.

compound—a substance in which the atoms of two or more elements combine and become something else. Sodium and chlorine will fuse to form salt, a totally different material.

corrosion—a process in which metal discolors and wears away because of a chemical reaction with oxygen in the air or water. The corrosion of iron produces rust.

ductile—easily drawn or dragged into long, thin shapes, such as gold wire.

electrum—a pale-yellow alloy of gold and silver. The name comes from the Greek word for "beaming sun."

element—any of more than one hundred basic substances that consist of atoms of only one kind. Each atom has a number of protons associated with it, which distinguishes it from all others.

filigree—a decorative technique using very fine wire of gold, silver, or copper.

fire assay—a method of estimating how much gold a sample of rocky material contains. The Egyptians first used it as a way to see whether there was enough gold in a region to mine it.

gilding—a process of covering an object with a thin layer of gold.

malleable—easily beaten or pressed into a desired shape.

matter—anything that takes up space and has mass.

precious metals—metals, such as gold, silver, and platinum, that are considered valuable or desirable because they are rare and strongly resist corrosion. They are also known as noble metals.

property—a quality or behavior that a substance displays.

Sources

Boyle, Robert W. *Gold: History and Genesis of Deposits.* New York: Van Nostrand Reinhold, 1987.

Brock, William H. *The Norton History of Chemistry.* New York: W. W. Norton & Company, 1992.

Cohen, Daniel. *Gold: The Story of the Noble Metal Through the Ages.* Philadelphia: Lippincott, 1976.

Hahn, Emily. *Love of Gold.* New York: Lippincott, 1980.

Heiserman, David L. *Exploring Chemical Elements and Their Compounds.* New York: TAB Books, 1992.

Hoving, Thomas. *Tutankhamen — The Untold Story.* New York: Simon and Schuster, 1978.

Hudson, John. *The History of Chemistry.* New York: Routledge, Chapman, & Hall., 1992.

Lyttle, Richard B. *The Golden Path.* New York: Atheneum, 1983.

Marks, Paula Mitchell. *Precious Dust. The American Gold Rush Era: 1848-1900.* New York: Morrow, 1994.

Meltzer, Milton. *Gold, the True Story of Why People Search for it, Mine It, Trade It, Steal It, Mint It, Hoard It, Shape It, Wear It, Fight and Kill for It.* New York: HarperCollins, 1993.

Newton, David E. *The Chemical Elements.* New York: Franklin Watts, 1994.

————*Secrets of the Alchemists.* Alexandria, Va.: Time-Life Books, 1990.

Vicker, Ray. *The Realms of Gold.* New York: Scribner, 1975.

Weeks, Mary Elvira. *Discovery of the Elements.* Easton, Pa.: Journal of Chemical Education, 1968.

Wheeler, Keith. *The Alaskans.* Alexandria, Va.: Time-Life Books, 1977.

Index

Italicized page numbers
indicate illustrations.

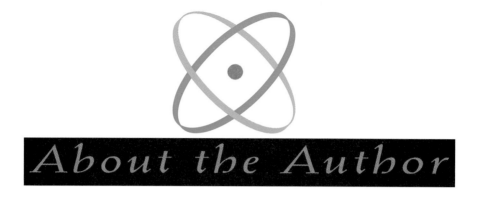

About the Author

Hal Hellman has a master's degree in physics from the Stevens Institute of Technology in Hoboken, New Jersey. He has been writing about science for adults and children for thirty years and is the author of twenty-seven books and many articles. He lives in Leonia, New Jersey, with his wife, Sheila.